EMMA JANE KIMMELL

Emma Jane Kimmell is a Seattle-based artist and graphic designer who is passionate about her work and about all things design. She specializes in drawing, painting, illustration, and freelance graphic design and has recently taken up web design. She started her project: *Sketch-A-Day* in 2011 and has been sketching every day since.

To see some of her daily sketches from this project, or if you're interested in commissioning or collaborating, please feel free to contact Emma Jane:

- instagram.com/emmajaneart
- www.emmajanedesign.com
- www.behance.net/ekimmell01a4
- www.linkedin.com/in/emmajanekimmell

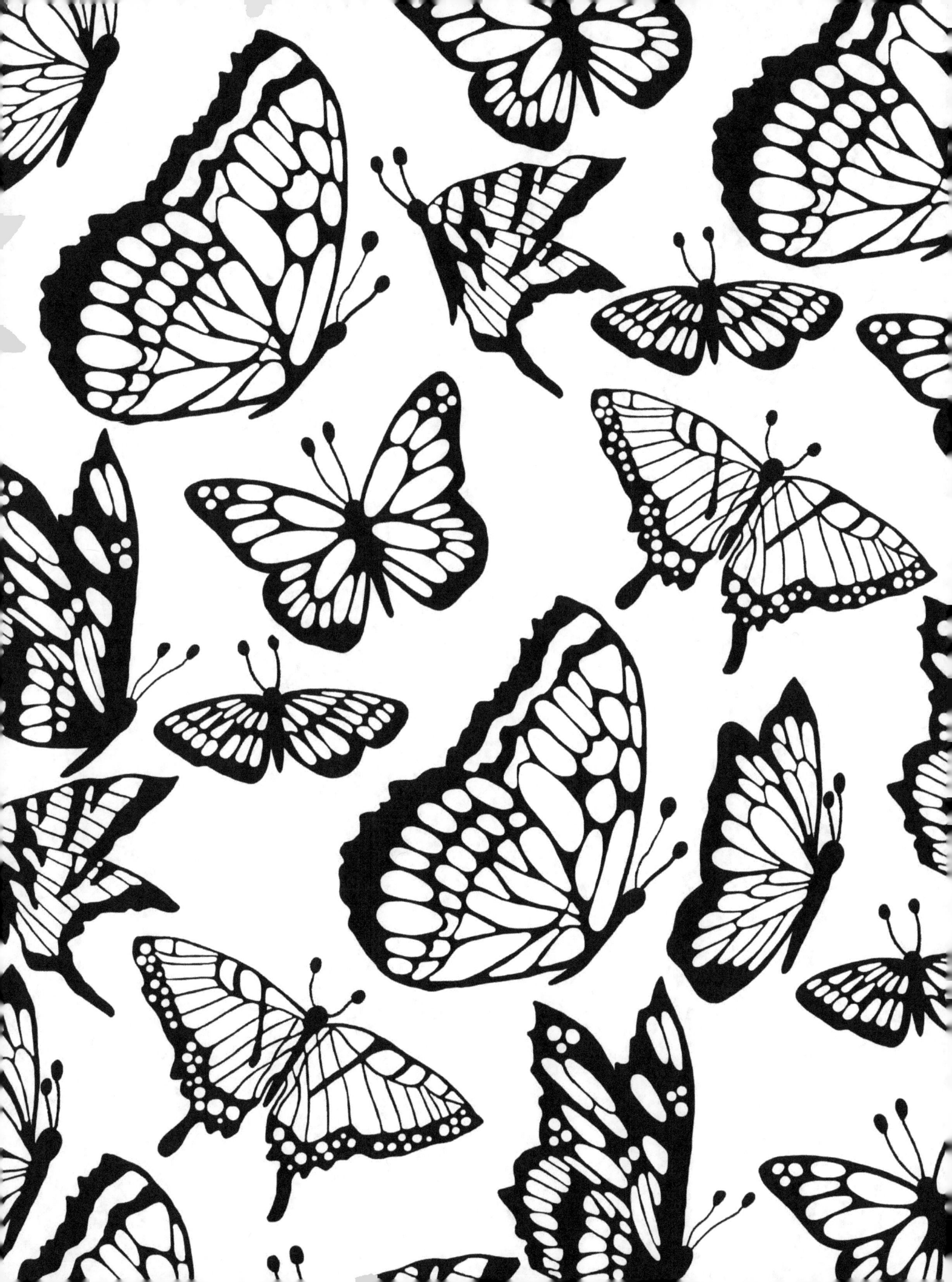

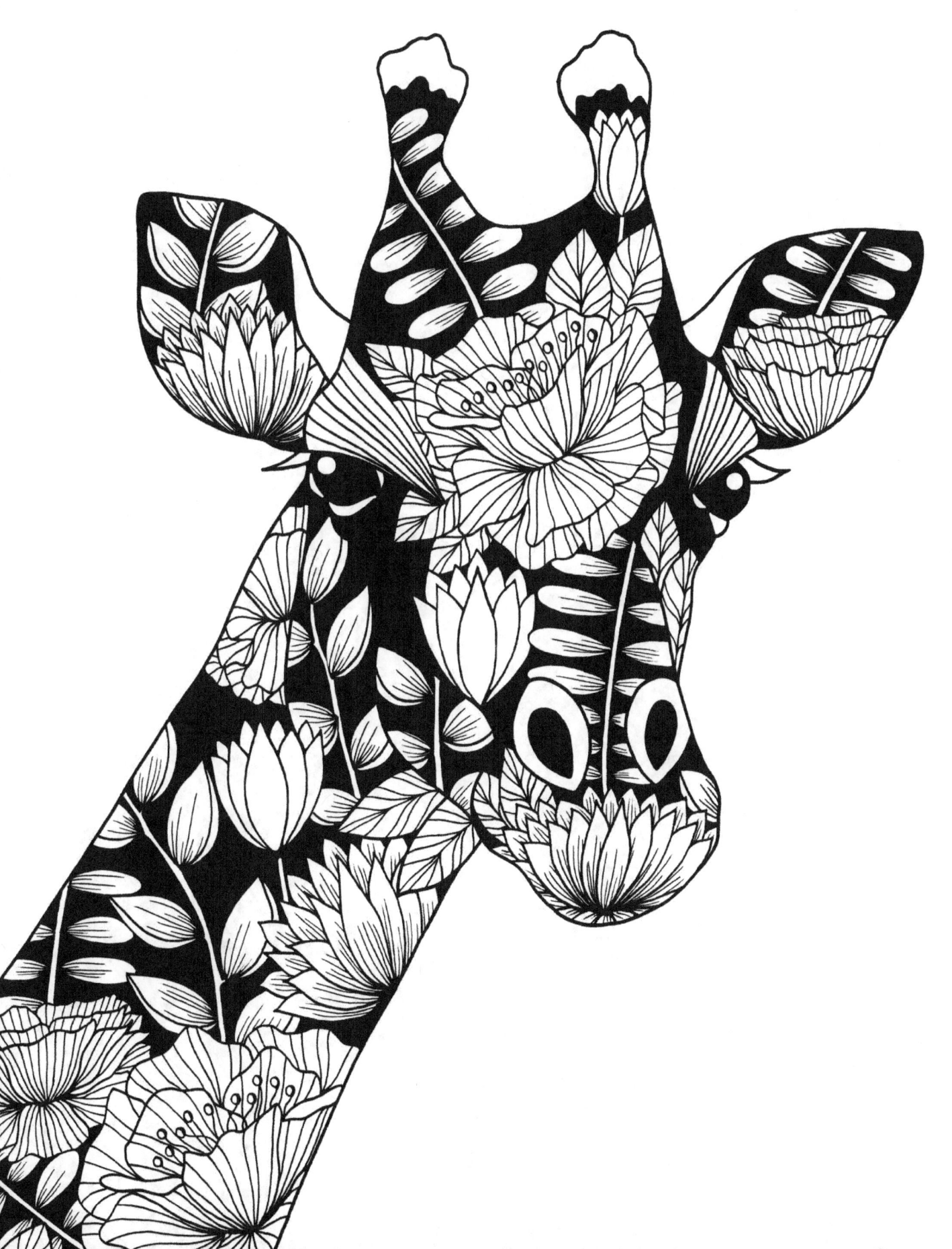

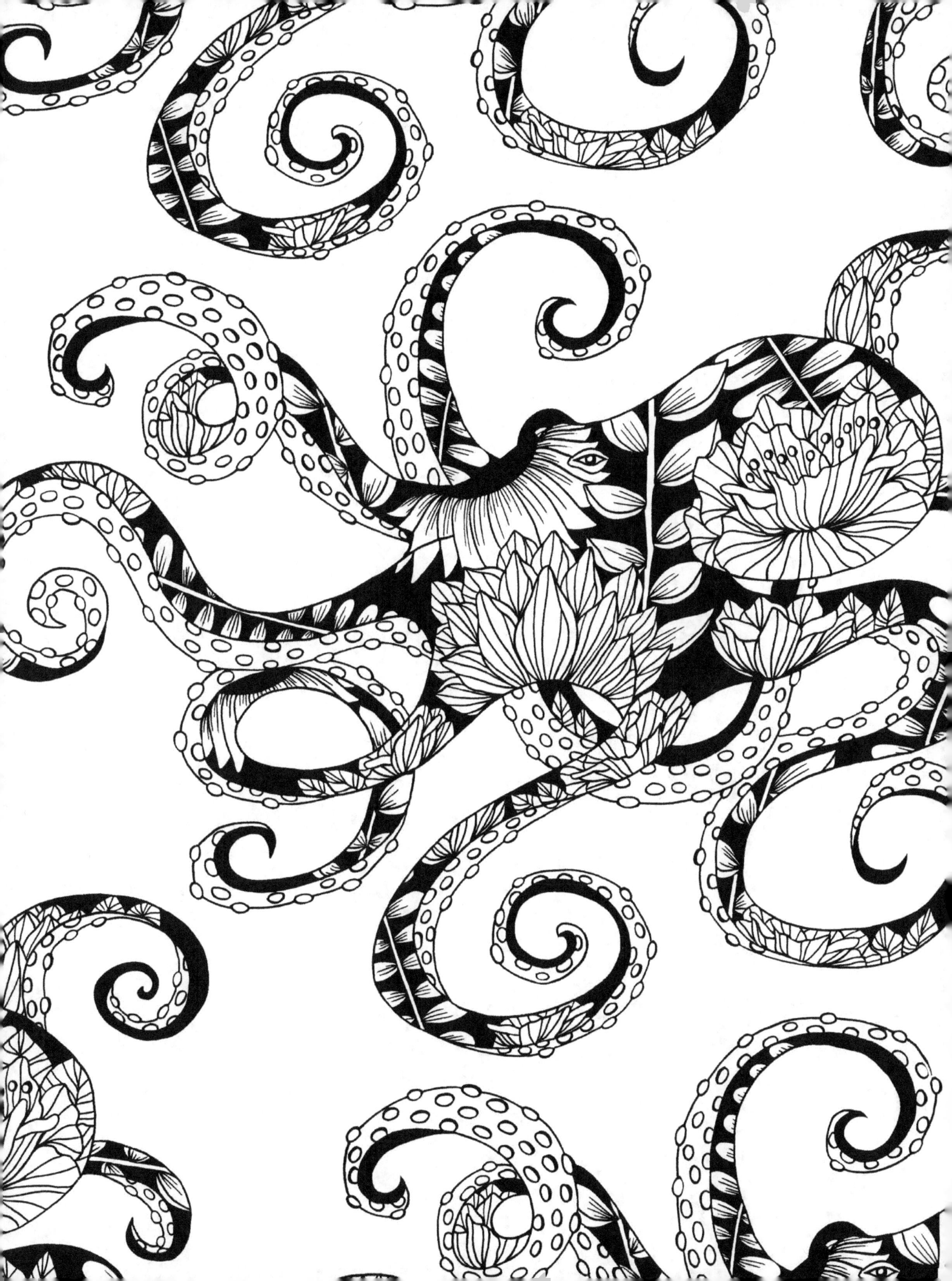

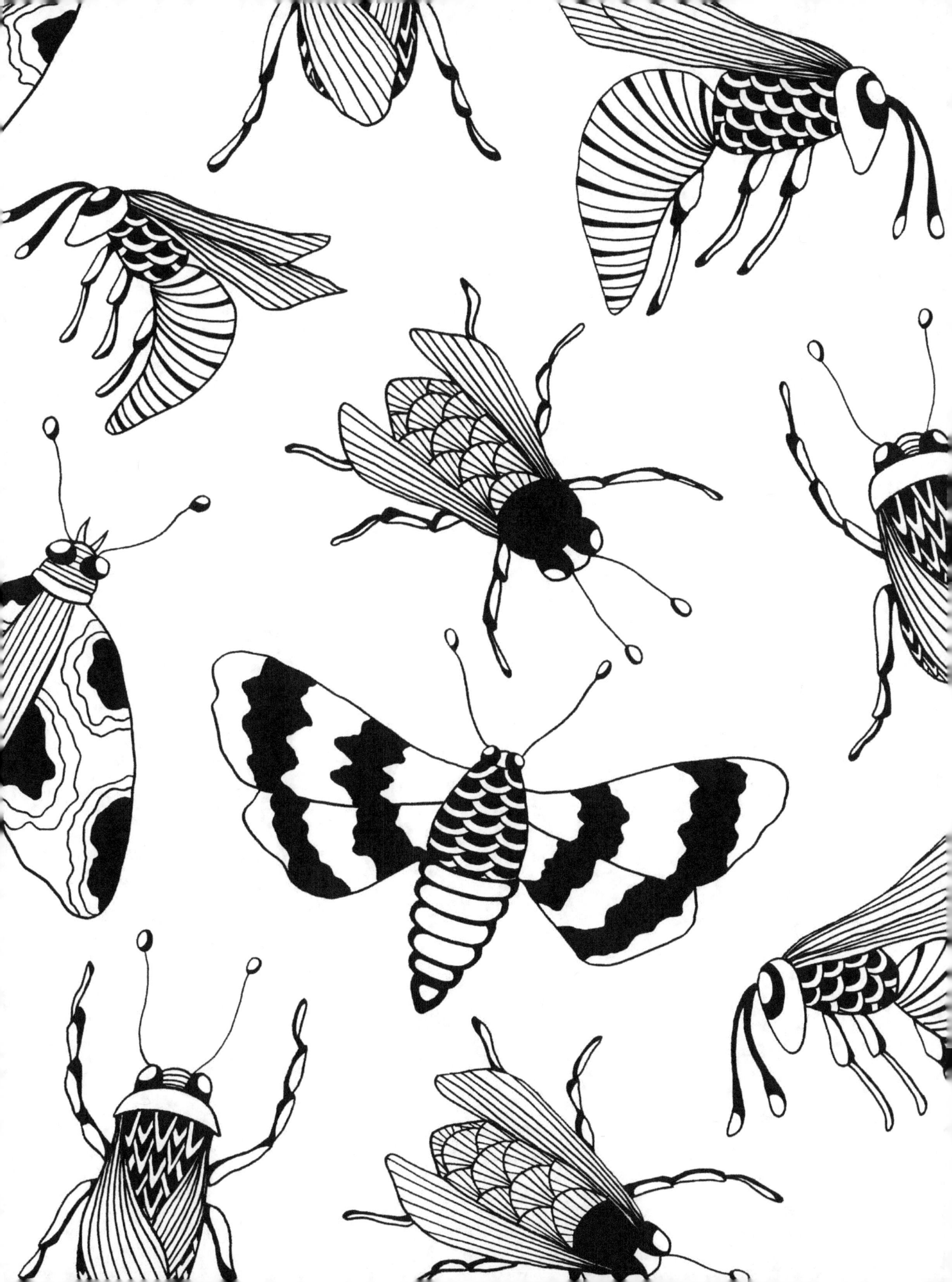

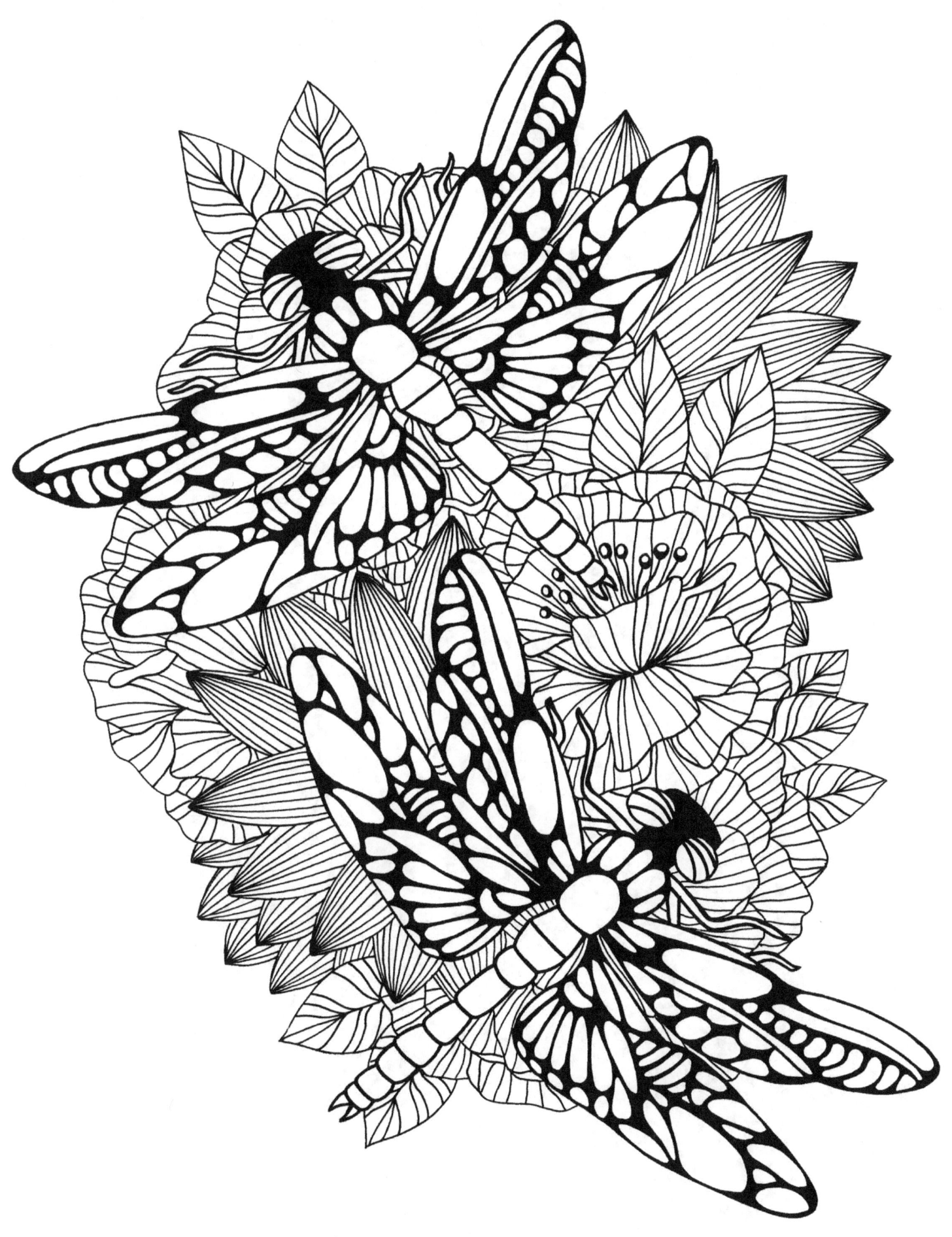

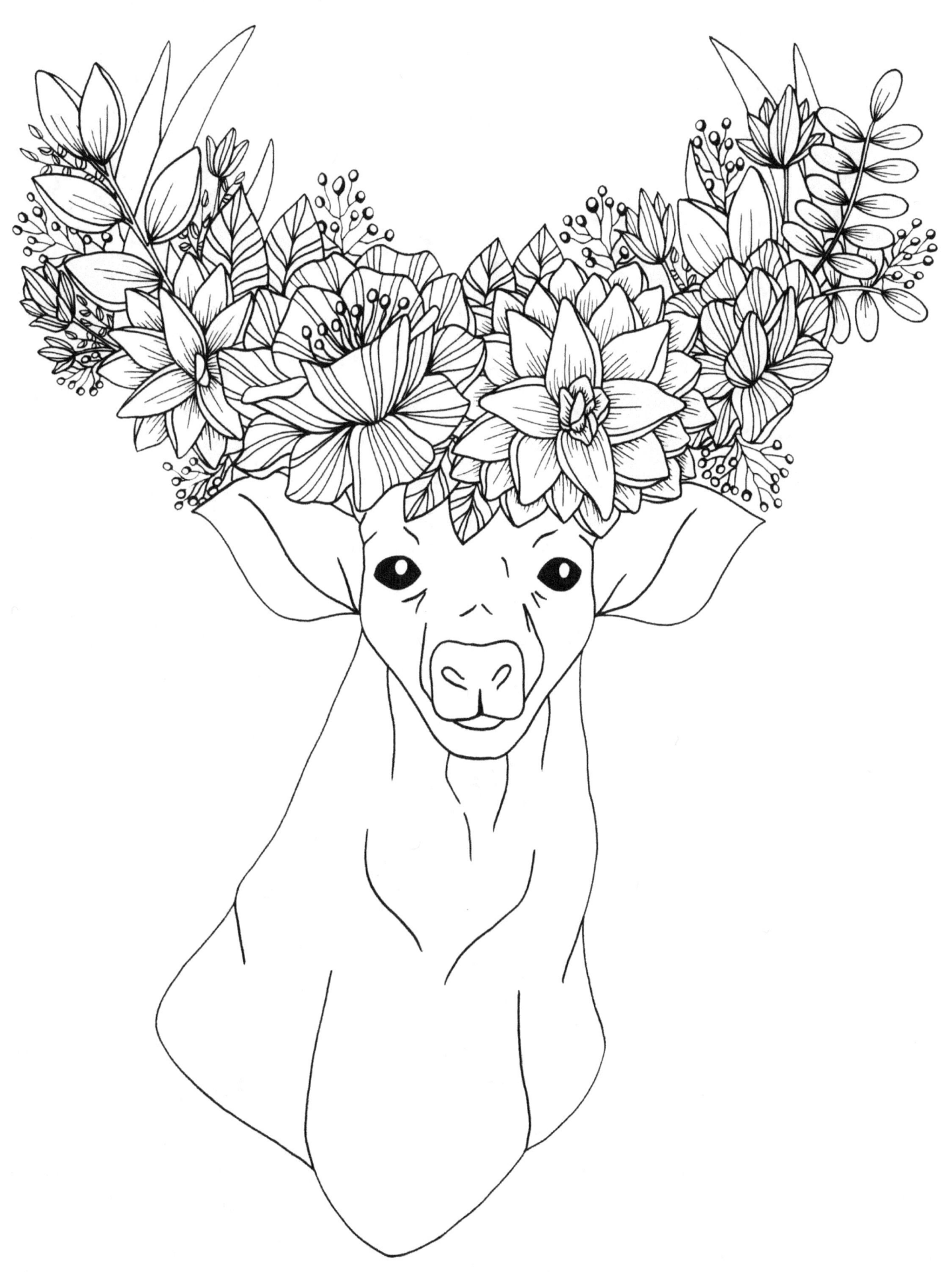

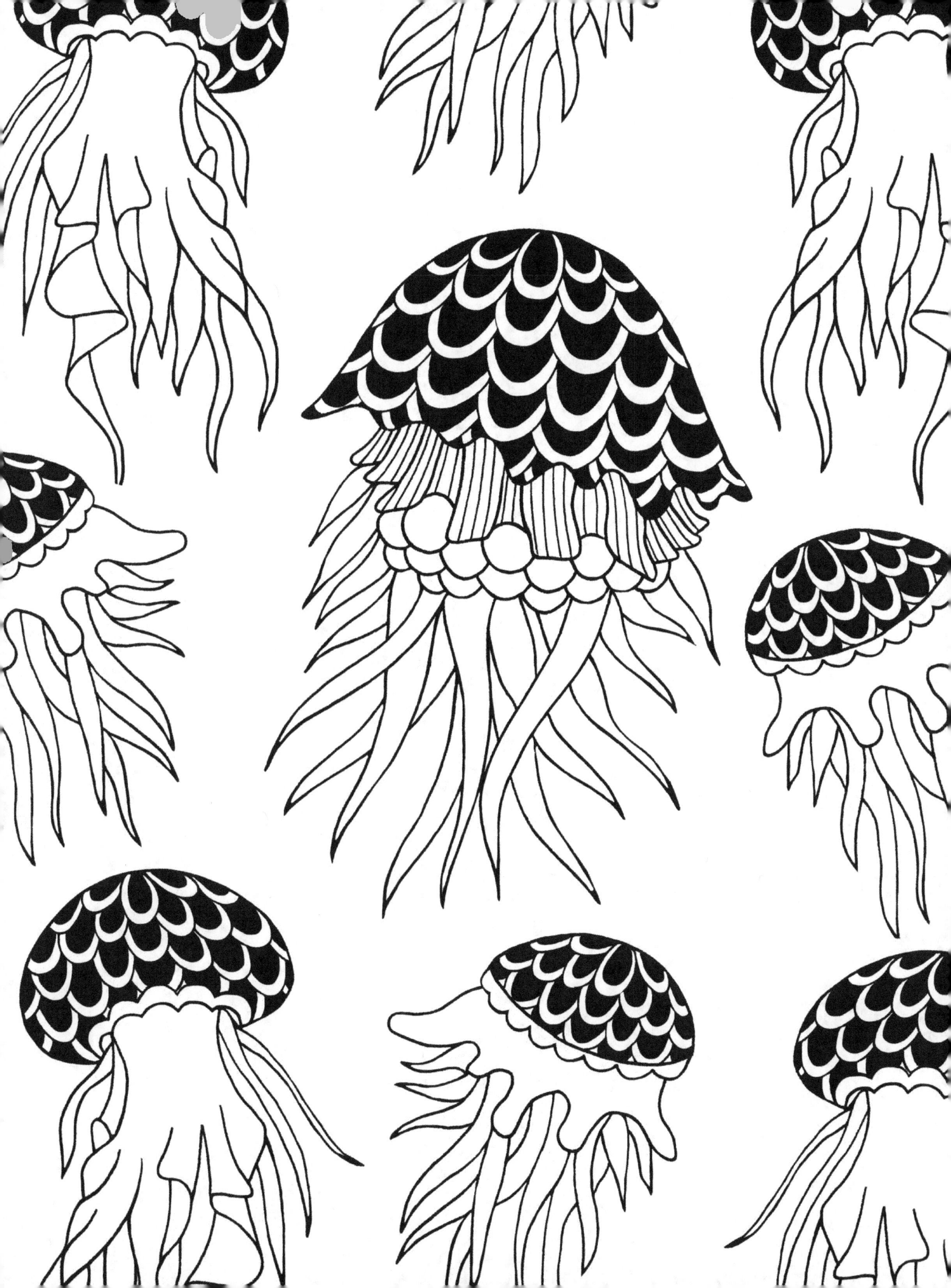

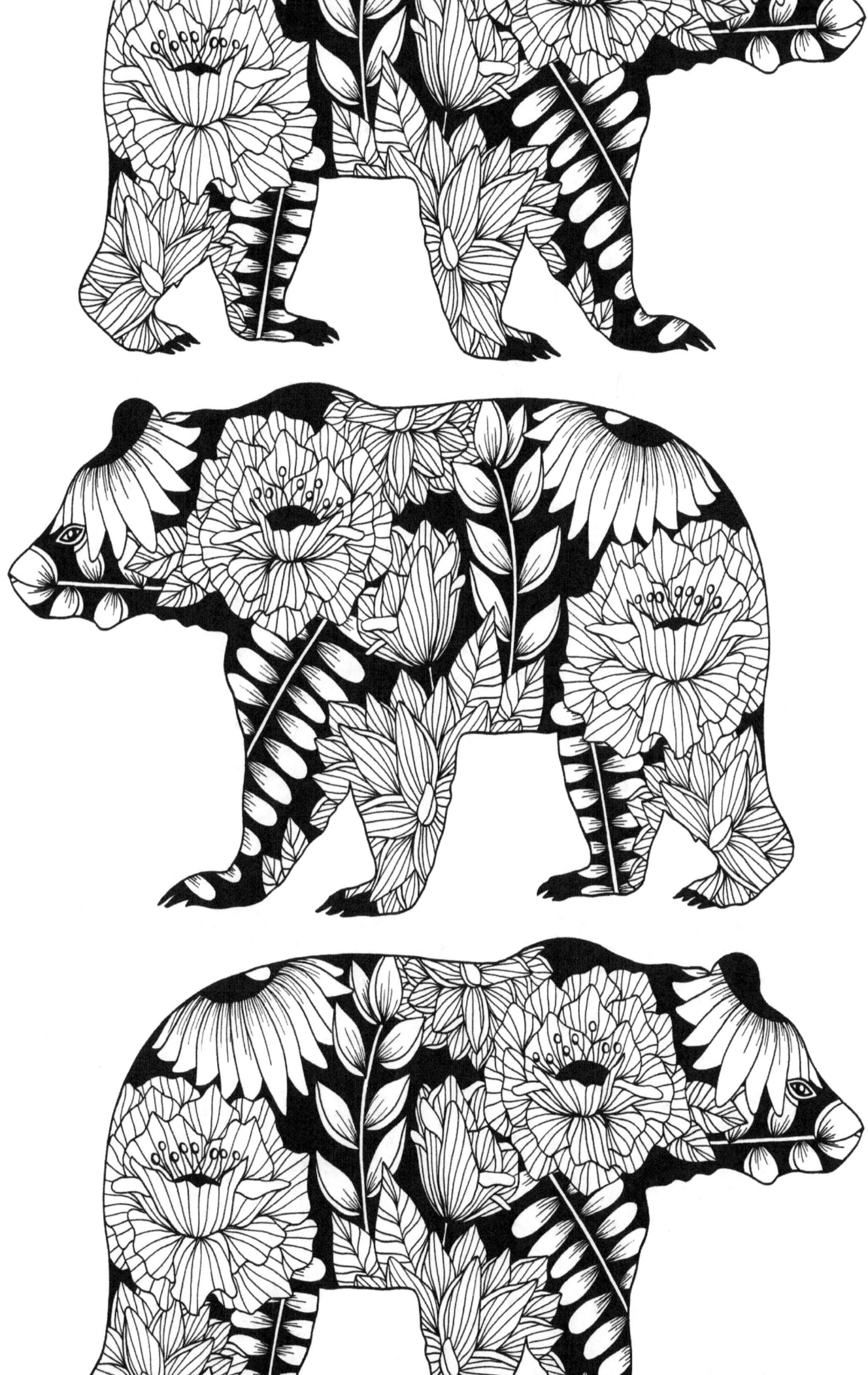

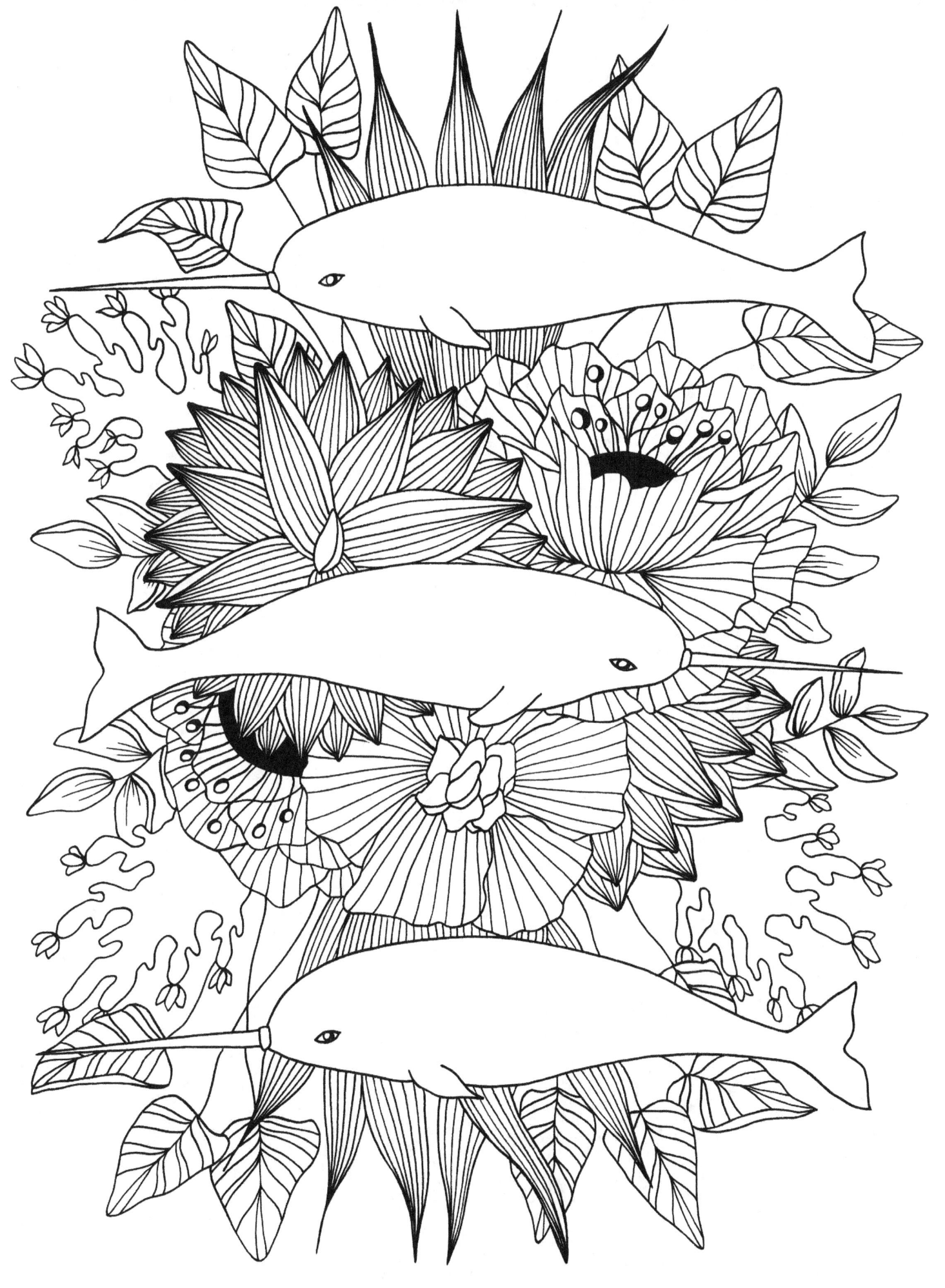

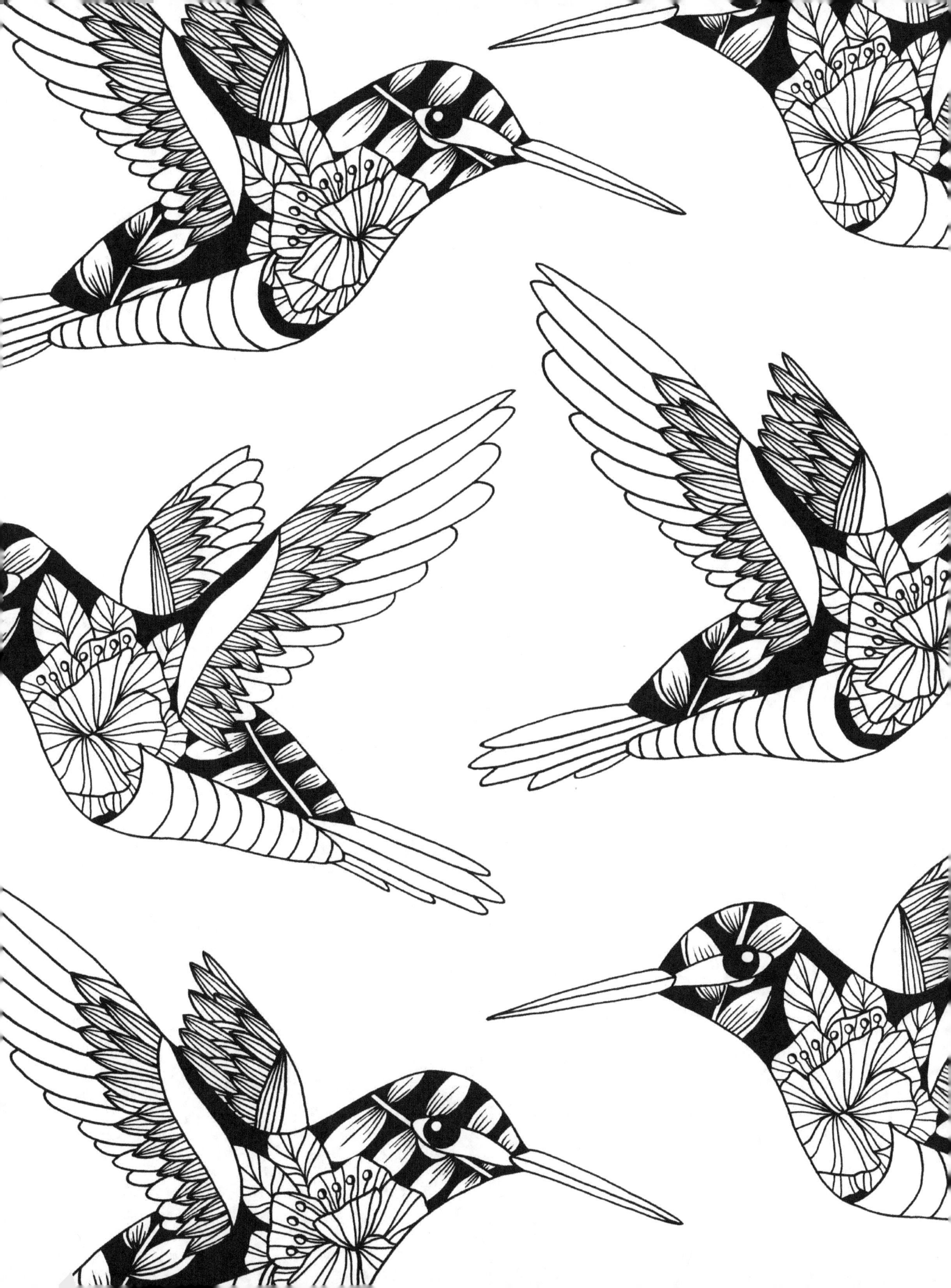

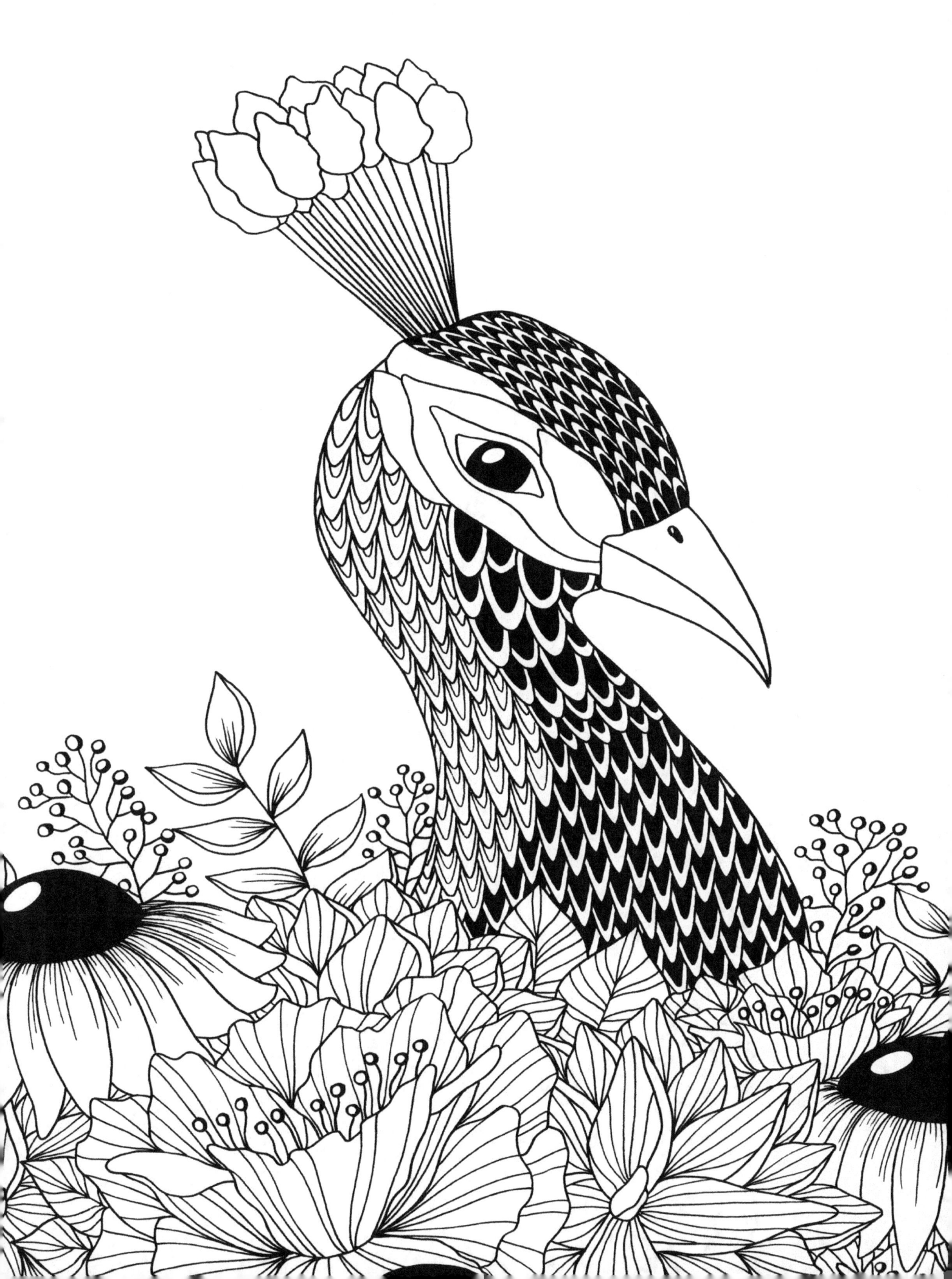

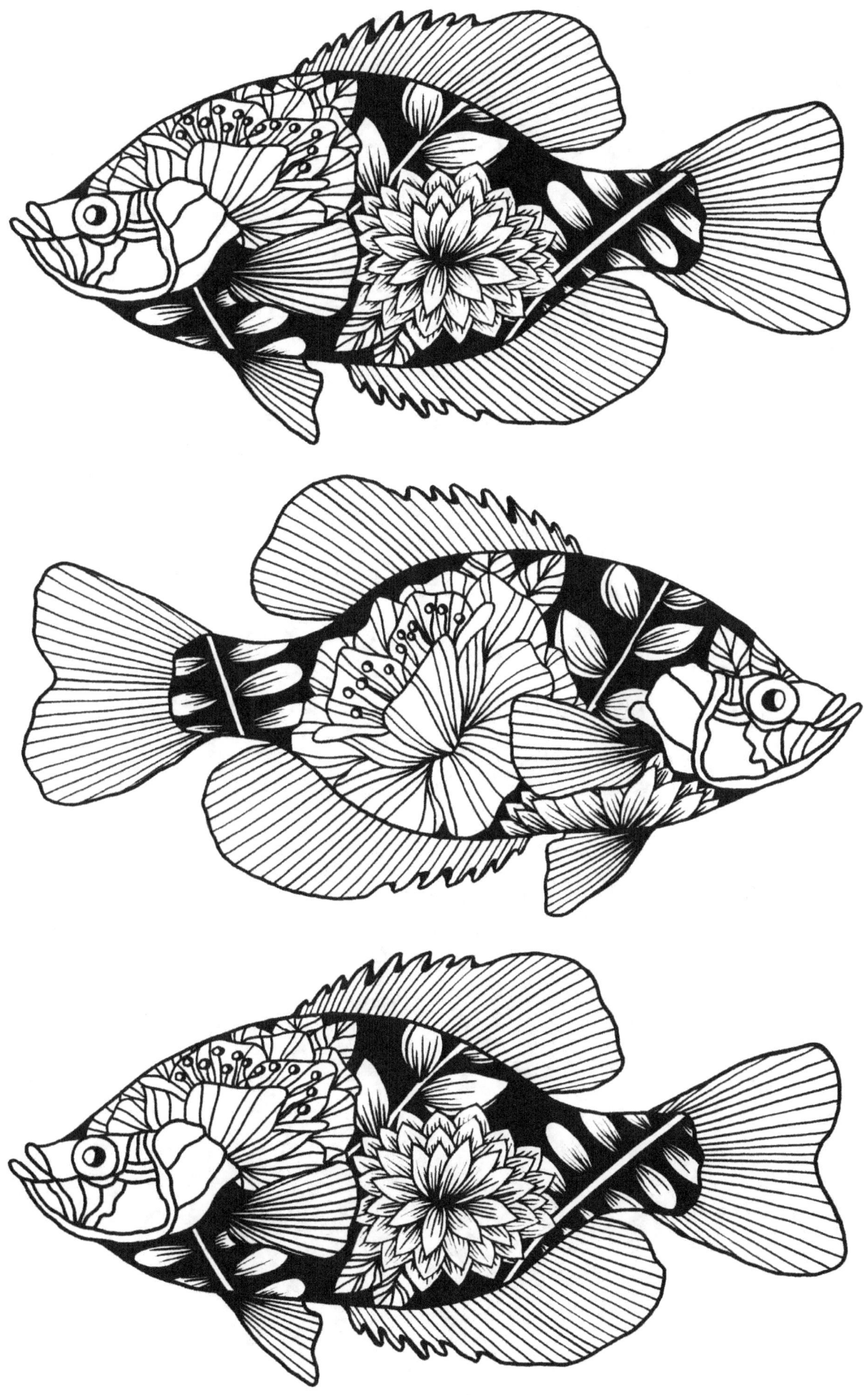

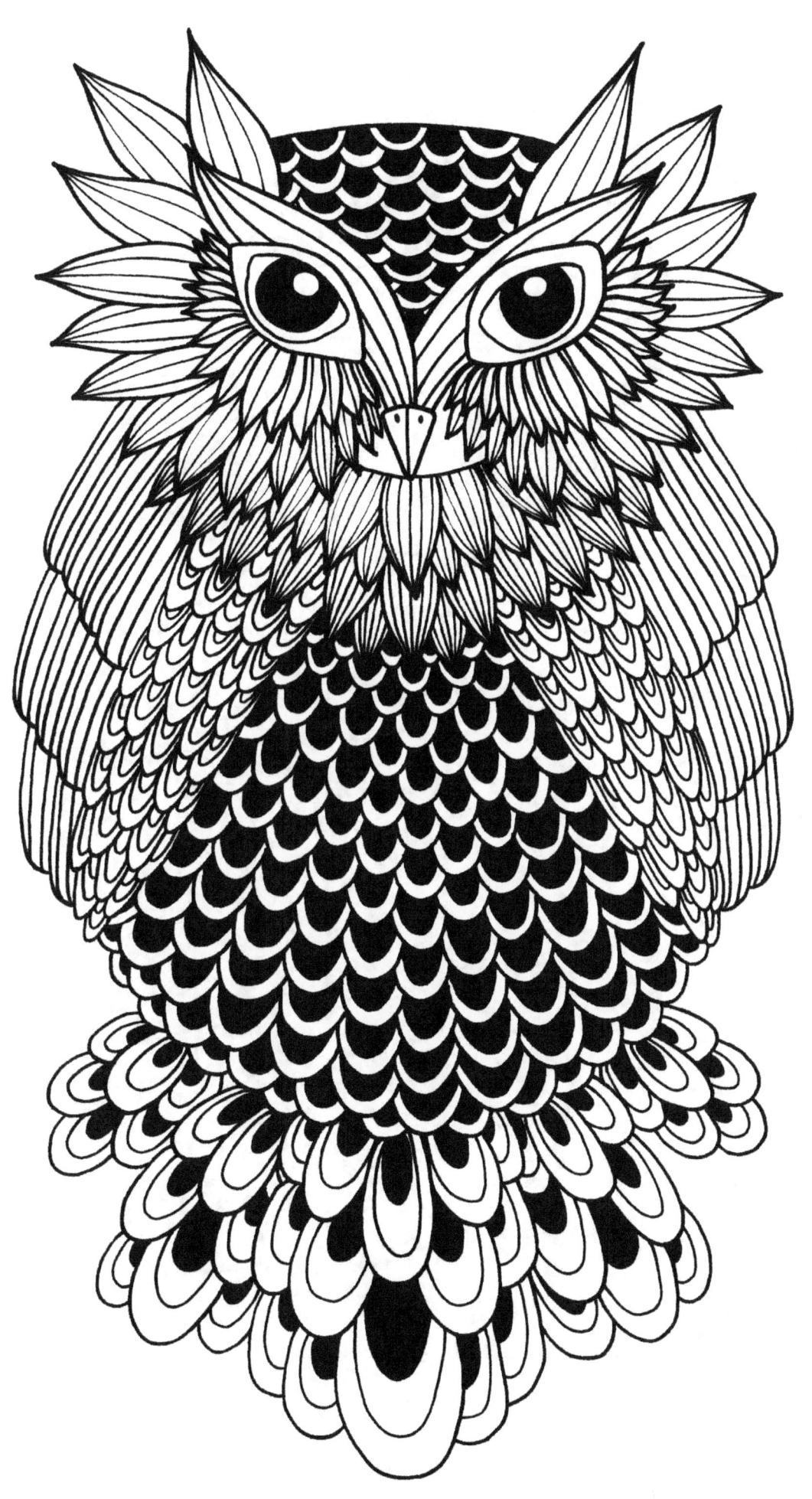

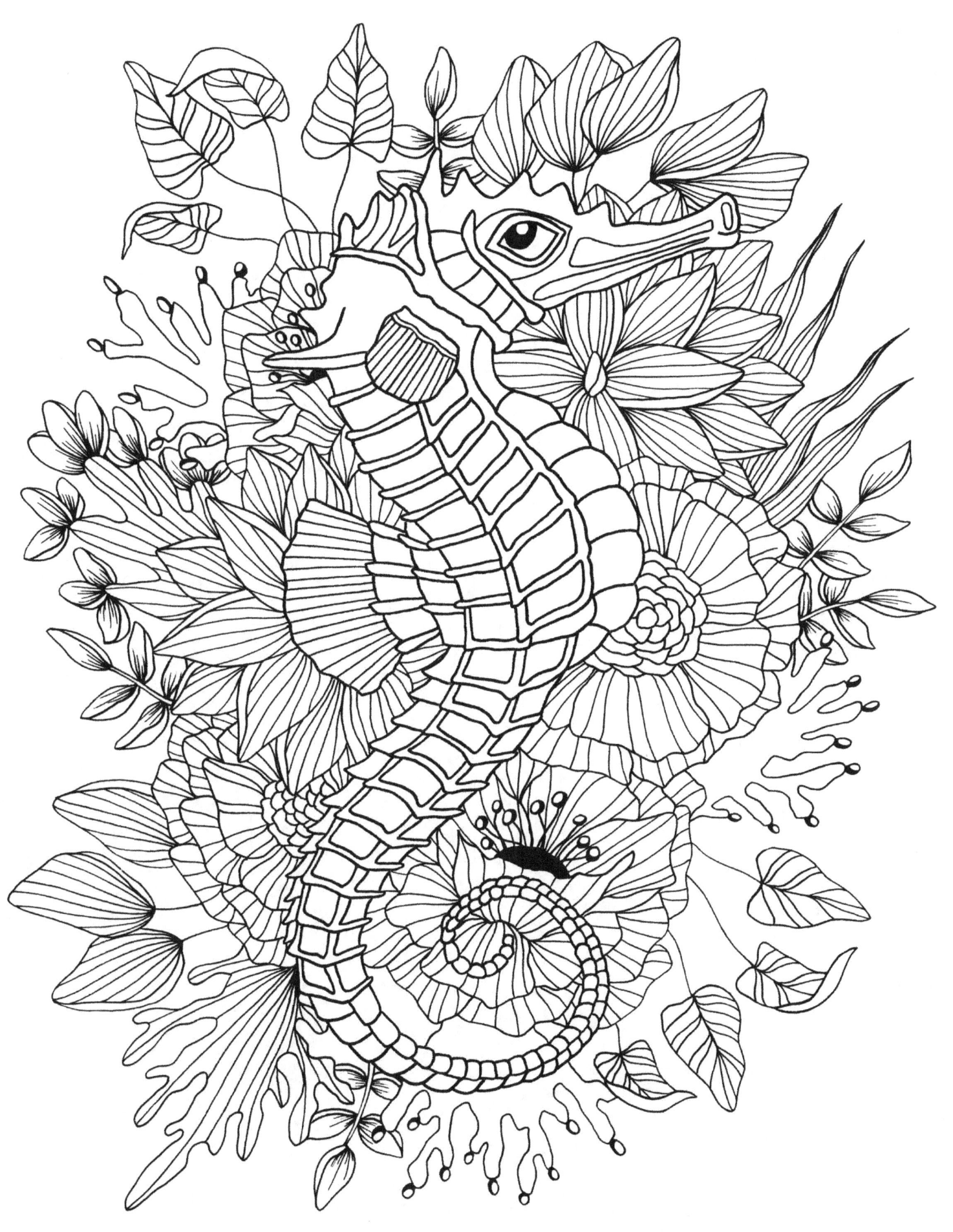

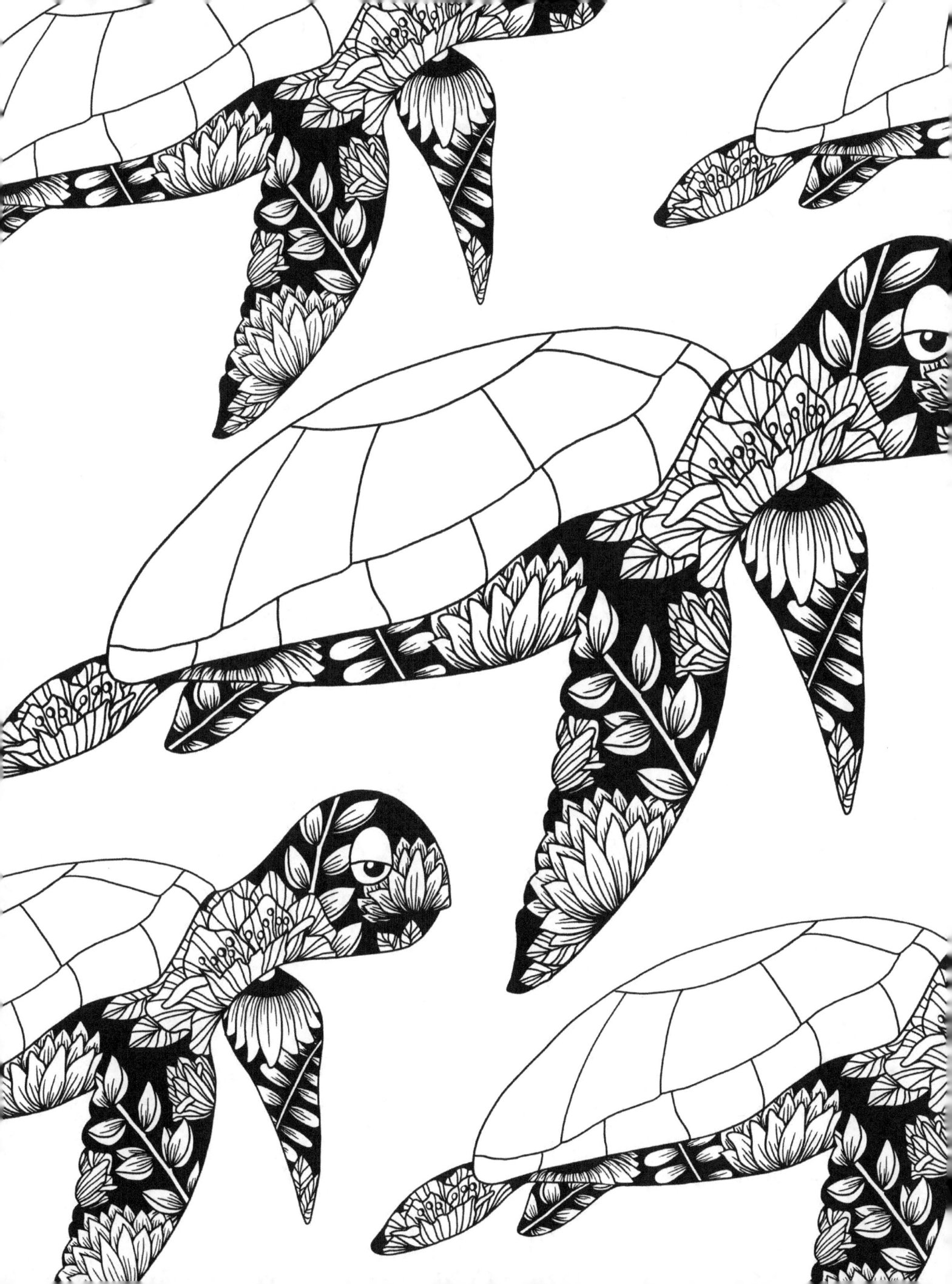

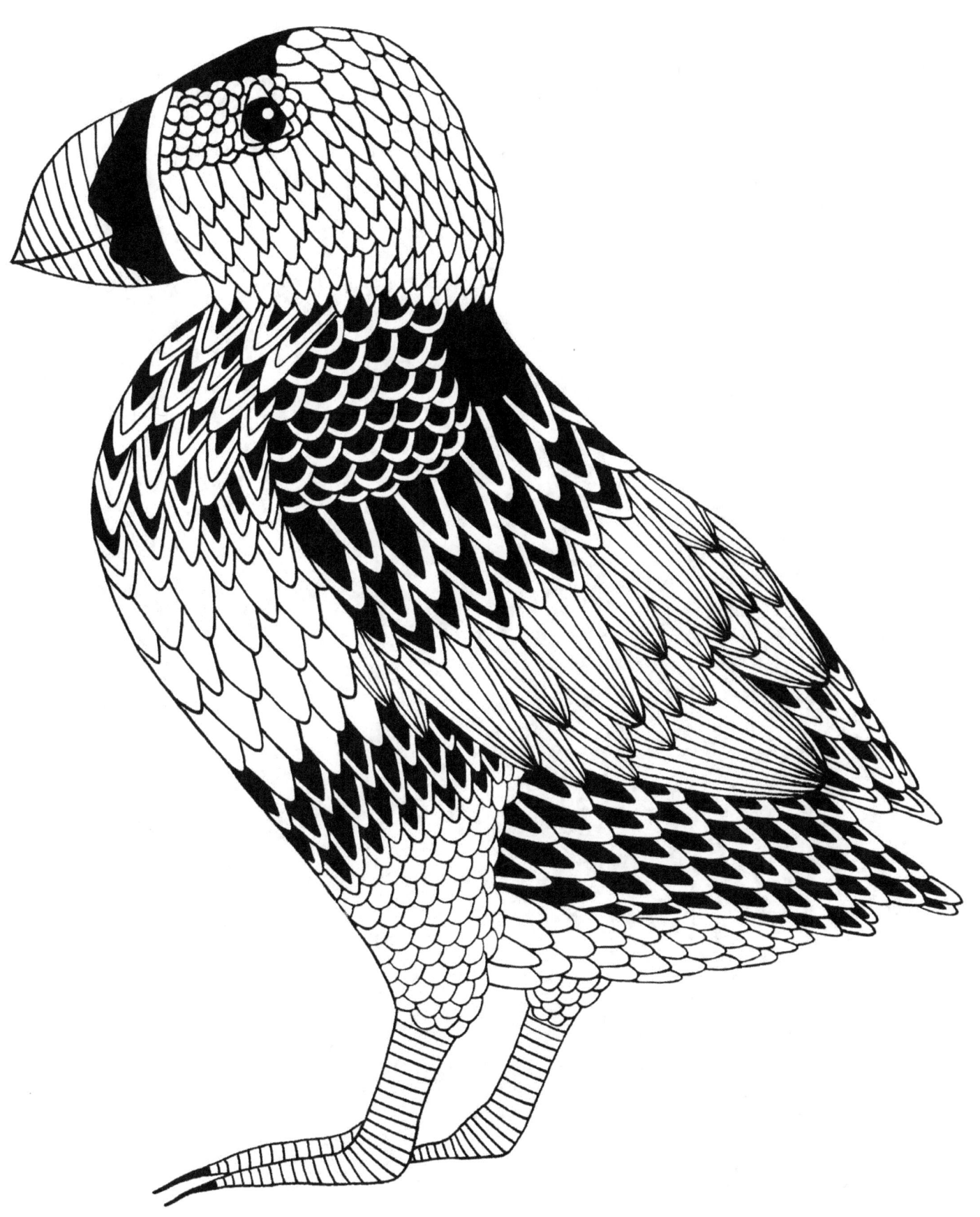

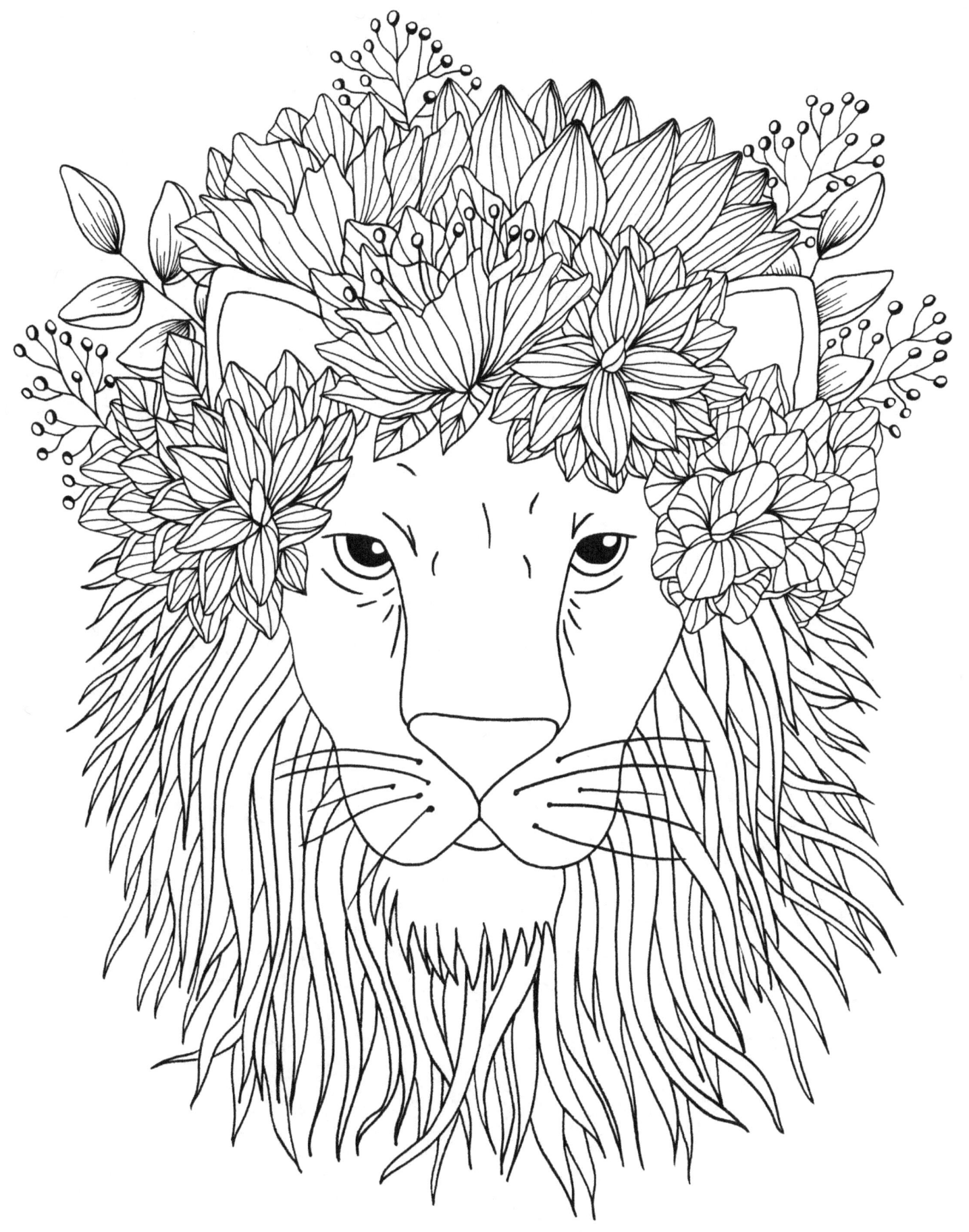

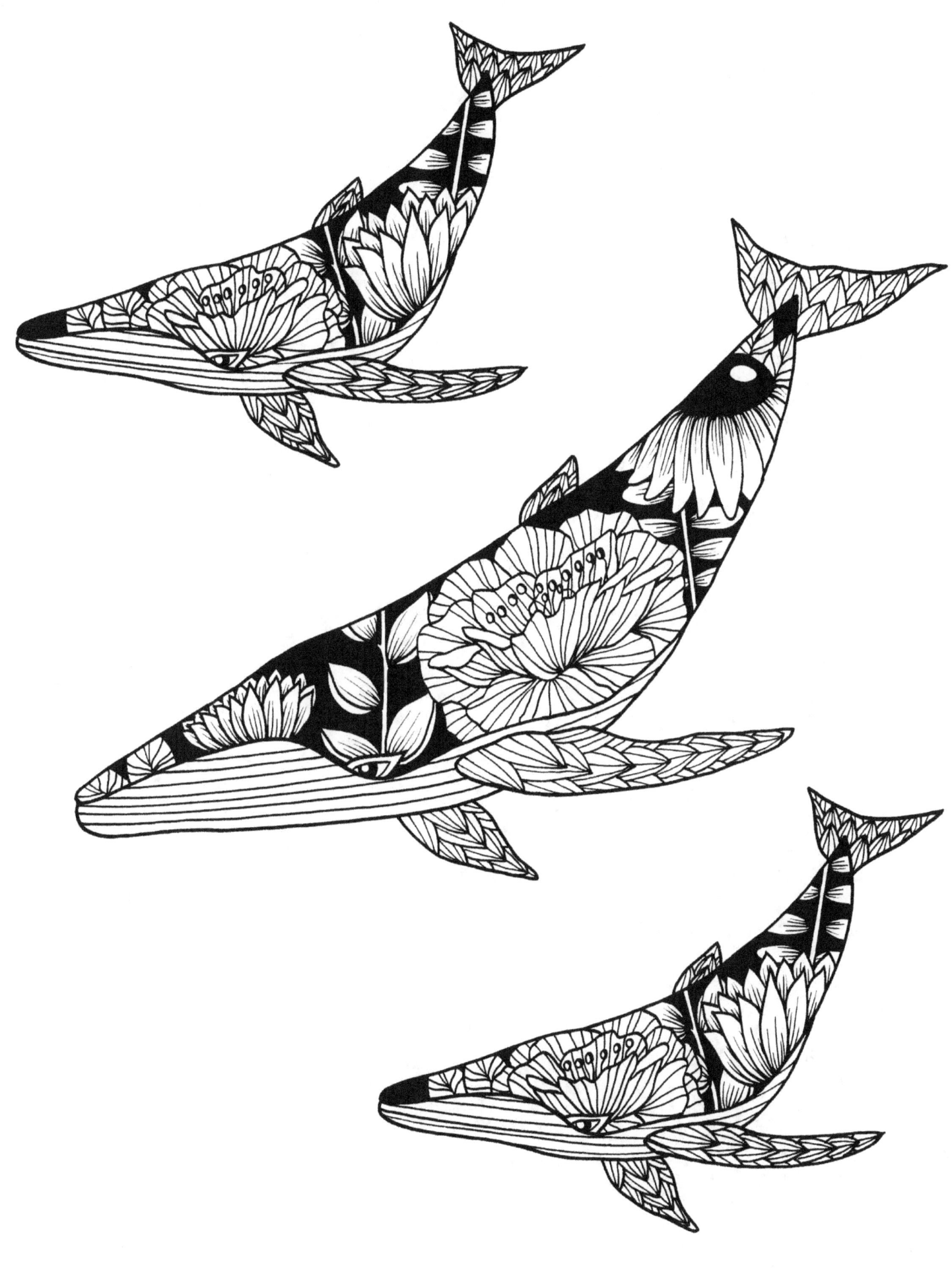

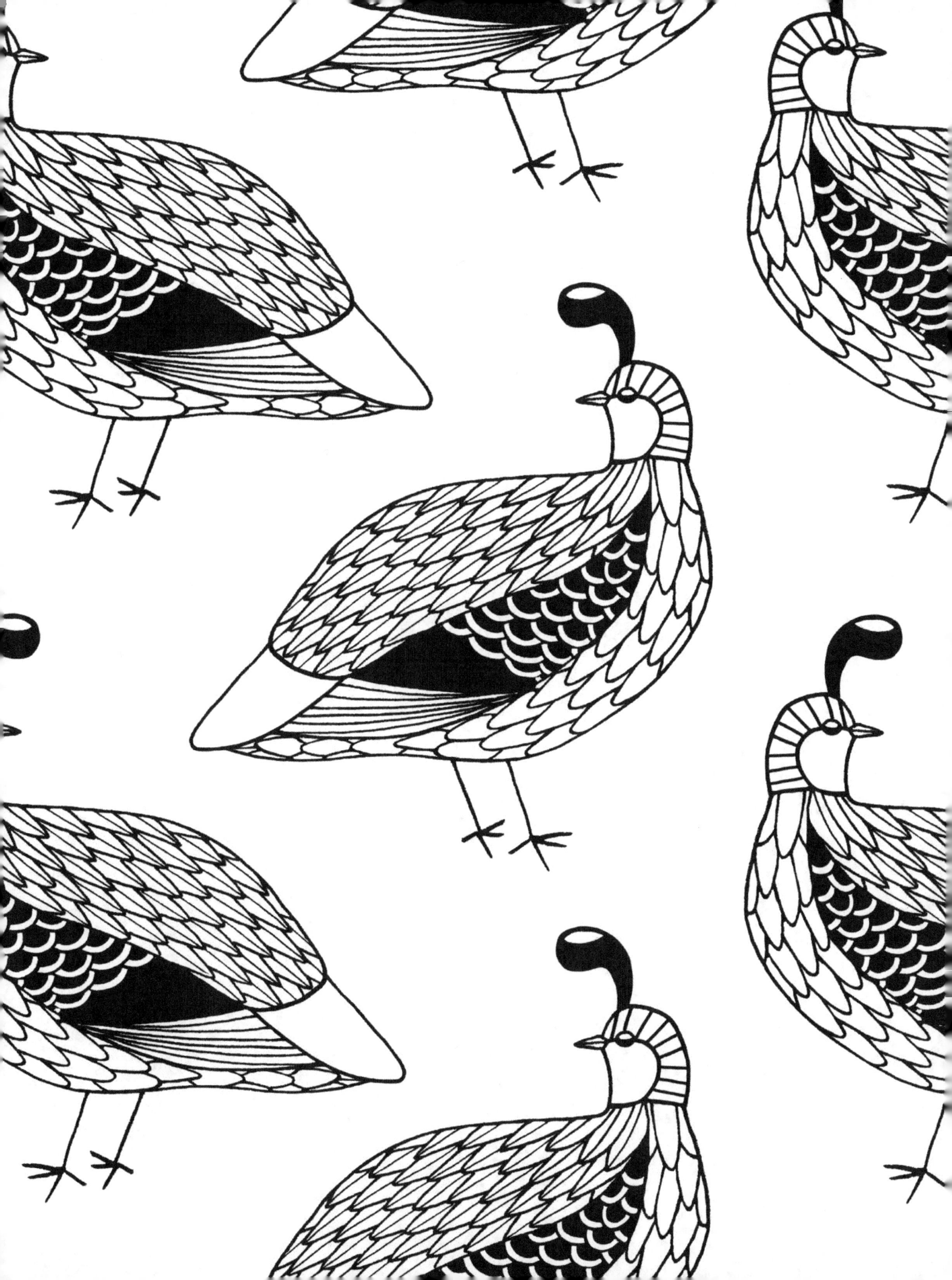

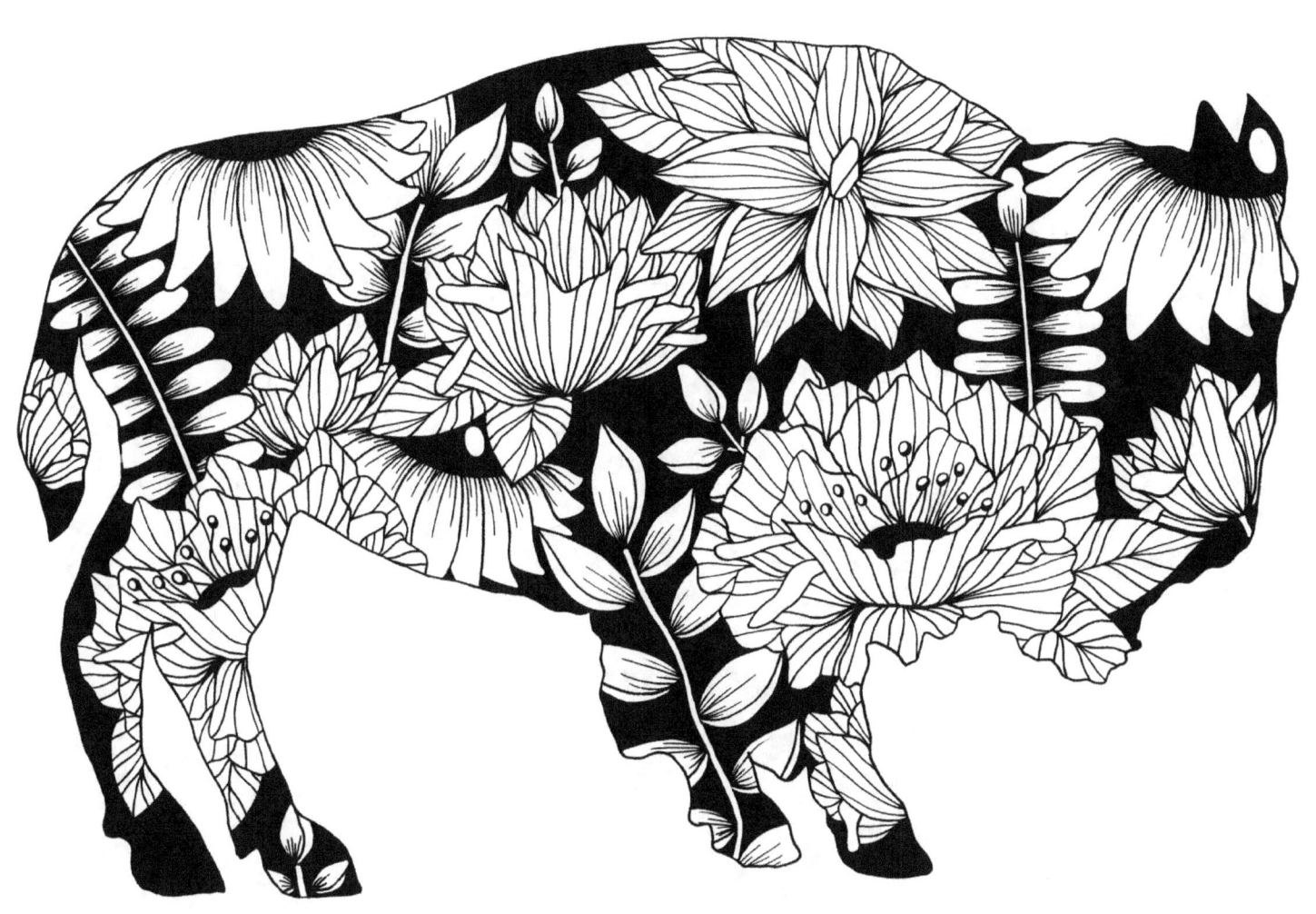

www.ingramcontent.com/pod-product-compliance
Lightning Source LLC
Chambersburg PA
CBHW062233220526
45471CB00009B/3461